The Indignation Parade

and

Other Poems

F. R. FOKSAL

The Indignation Parade
and
Other Poems

The Nonconformist Press

The Nonconformist Press

To my muse,
Dorothy

ABOUT THE AUTHOR

F. R. Foksal is a Polish author, poet, and critic writing in English, as well as the founder of the literary magazine, *The Nonconformist*.

Contents

———

Indignation

A Slice of Surreality

a shortcut
you used to take,
located somewhere
between a fatigued
façade and a bench

bare; a cozy little square
where local drunks would
congregate to damn
the vicissitudes
of their tipsy

fate; a hole in the fence
through which you peeked
under the lining
of the world till then
impenetrable and

still; a hunchbacked tree
from under the cover
of whose leaves
it took you
all your childhood

to flee; a tank's caterpillar
tread on your doorstep—
in life, the only one
that would never yield
a butterfly

In the Cellar

an old bicycle
limping on one wheel,
laminated with
the sheer silk
of cobwebs; a pile
of potatoes huddling
in the corner,
in the back—a steep
hill unmarked
on any map; a cardboard
box full of books
never opened, their spines
never cracked, still virginal
and yet gray with age,
covered with a thick
stubble of dust, dead
in their youth; a shy stain
on the wall—will the ceiling
hold up when the bombs
start to fall

Ode to the Trenches

there's a rain that sandblasts
the walls; there's a rain that reopens

old wounds; there's a rain that
carries our names to the clouds;

there's a rain in which we suffer
as the only ones; there's a rain that

you can hear after years in the desert
spent; there's a rain that squeezes

into the eyes of blind men;
there's a rain that you ponder on

before falling asleep; there's a rain
for which only wily willows weep;

there's a rain that makes other rains
look still; and there's a rain in which
people learn to kill

The Silence of the Loudest Scream

the loneliness of the wind leafing
through a book in a bombed-out room

is almost as moving as the morning
catching fright from the horizon all alight;

the scream of shot-through glass
in a toothless window frame

is almost as acute
as the limping of a table lame;

the modesty of a doll stripped
of a flood of frills by fire tongues

is almost as strange as the world
that I will never know

Under the Eaves

how to piece together a pavement
from a paving slab puzzle
so that old ladies
don't trip over it
while walking with
their puppies to a bakery to buy
their rolls' every-morning
supply; how to paint bollards
so that there are no stains, no gripe,
and that there is no doubt which
stripe is which; how to build a bench
so that children don't ride on it
like on a snotty playground slide;
and how to make such little things,
not on a par with math problems, last
when the world around them
goes up in a blast

The Words

hundreds of authors
with millions of words
have already described
all shades of evil,
broken down
into flavors,
types and shapes,
models and kinds,
and yet again,
today, just look,
in a newspaper
the ink is black
like dried blood

A Silent Witness

who has seen more barbarity,
more acts depraved, more
abuses of power, all grievous
and grave, throughout the centuries
piled on top of each other, like
sounds on a stave, and yet
chose to stand aside, aloof,
an impartial observer not interested
in any trial, in any proof—the sky's apathy
is the cruelest of all

Biding One's Time

remember the well
the coin dived into, deep, deep,
remember the little boy
leaning over its edge when
he couldn't sleep, remember the sound
the pebble made taking the plunge, the plash,
remember the girls giggling
at the foolish folk tales about
wells and monsters, monsters
and lairs, remember how you yearned
to glimpse the reflection of her hair,
remember the time when its bottom
was poor, remember that now it sparkles
with gold as a New Year's coiffure,
remember how you feared to fall
like a little pebble down the well's throat,
remember the tightness, the closeness
of walls, remember the fall that never was,
remember these people pulled out of the well
on the paper's front page, their dead
bodies blurred to spare us their stare,
remember them well

In the Dark Room

this or that dark outline conceals
a power of possibilities untold,

like a treasure trove of shapes,
figures, and forms, which

at a mere glance releases
a throng of threats, visions,

and promises, when
this chair is a castle, that pile of clothes

is a hill, though planted on a table,
and the door of a closet

becomes an unclimbed gable, on top
of which a beast lurks,

or two, but there are places in the world
where horrors are true

The Pulse of Progress

gigabytes of dreams,
an unsifted stream, along
with gigahertz and gigawatts
of progress pulsate through
a maze of cables, through
wires filled to the brim, bringing
mirth and tears, thrills and
making mute minds sing,
within the same second, across
the globe's girdled girth, across
this cultures and languages'
melting pot, but today, just
like a hundred years before,
the victims in mass graves
are left to rot, shot through
their heads, like dummies
sporting in their hair hairpins
made of maggots and mold;
they crowd within the space
not wide enough to park
a scooter in another corner
of the world; but here the soil
is the final bedclothes
they are forced to endure,
deep in the forest, among
the tombstones of trees, where
time has stopped, and where
barbarity reigns pure

In the Beginning Was the End

the iron bars and iron walls
dotted with the bars

of tally marks entomb
a soul, no less steely than

the will of a prison guard,
than his baton hard, than his

helmet, than his cap, than his
uniform black with apathy

dried, or is it justice,
justice it must be, they claim,

but there are stains
that no bleach can banish,

as there always remains
a morsel, so much as a morsel,

of beliefs' blend that in the beginning
of everything was the end

The Indignation Parade

but then I saw
indignation in its purest
form

distilled in their mouths
the ovens of
rage

leaving their bodies
soaring up into
the sky

souls launched with
the advent of the last
sigh

the miniature
kites

a forest of fists I saw
hovering over their
heads

once tucking their
children
in

each fist the size
of an extracted
heart

the empty nests
in a chocolate
box

but as they passed me I saw
my hand
trembling

a vacillating fly
uncertain whether
it should stay

    fly away

        or die

The Point of Exclamations

the silent scream of the masses,
the avalanche of exclamation marks

are the only forms of communication left
when the last bastion of dialogue falls,

when its towers are trampled on,
when there's a breach glaring

in its weighty walls, when its front
gate gapes open, a void

torn in its face, now aghast, a mortal
wound, only then are we brought

to the threshold, to the point
of no return ripe with protest signs

answering prayers unanswered
resolving issues unresolved,

only then are we led to no man's land
that no explorer has set a spying foot in,

for the immediacy of a threat
calls for the immediacy of a battle cry,

and only then are we nearing,
in an effort just, the critical mass,

the point of exclamations
full of rage and disgust

The Peripheral Vision

at times I feel
the phantom of fear gallop
through my veins,

tenebrous and tight,
and then

take the left turn, take the right
one and staunchly refuse to stop,
refuse to obey the pleadings

of a mind desperate
for a crumb of
normalcy revived, for

the appeals of common sense
striving to broker a peace
deal,

to patch up the holes
in the fabric of my dignity
unraveled,

dappled with doubts,
lingering like the first fall of snow,
impassive and benign,

as I watch the horrors
of horrors hoard up within
the tabernacle of a TV

screen
and rap silently
on the other side

of its surface lustrous
like fiery fangs
inside a hearth,

sizzling,
seething in me,
though unable

to hurt any part
of me
yet

The Taste of Marble

the color of marble,
so noble—
adorning columns
dressed up in the Greek fashion;
meandering on the floors
of temples and bank halls,
these two places of worship
so similar, so alike,
among mahogany inlays;
immortalizing great figures
enchanted in graceful poses
by a chisel in a sculptor's hand,
that primitive photographer;
decorating vaults and offices—
is a sign of status and splendor,
of shameless wealth,
and in the end, a simple lid
guarding the place
of final rest;
the belated taste
of luxury
for the poor

The Patron Saint of Sinners

hypocrisy of the rich
is stunning if you see
from whom they got
their wealth
to begin with

the poor hands and poor souls
let alone poor sweat of the poor
are needed to grow
a portico, a pillar, a porch
and their shade cool

an acre of comfort is worth
two ounces of woe,
three grains of gloom,
fours spoons of sorrow,
or misery in full bloom

A View Through the Fogged-up Glasses

we are passing by,
ships in the fog,

keeping their distance,
obeying their course,
calling out

like whitetail whales,
this undersea aristocracy,
in the dialect of

formal fog
horns, going in and out
of focus, time and again

clinging to one another,
yet afraid of
a touch,

ships in the fog,
we are passing by

The Return of the Queen

out of horrors
out of misery
born is the queen's
unforeseen return;

the tide of time
flows backward as
the unsheathed claws,
as the spiked horns

replace the now-silent
horns of cars unwept,
unsung, and unmourned;

paw after paw,
claw after claw,
the long-banished queen
regains her

footing in the dominions
long lost and long
stolen from her,

as the legs of her
minions march
and efface

the footprints
of this civilization
no longer missed,
even if unburied

still and weak;
no more than a week
was needed

to fill the canals,
the squares,
and the streets,

now deserted by everyone
but the new plague,
with animals wild,
with dolphins long unseen,

celebrating the return
of the once-exiled
queen

The Pilgrimage

the end of an epoch
that has started as

a seismic shift
ends drowned in the sea

of irrelevance and
passes unnoticed—

a pawn fallen
on the battlefield

of a chequered game;
a tree toppled

at the forest's doorstep,
again—as its bards and its acolytes

now busy donning
their new plumage

set out on a long
pilgrimage as if

following the migratory
timetables of birds

to be absolved of their sins
of their blunders bold

for to err
is easy I am told

The Nomad

the general march of changes
and the changing of the guard

are not to be challenged
or disputed, yet I can see

them walk in a circle
more vicious than

the most vile of devices
a human kind can contrive;

following in the footsteps
of sunspots they spin

like grounds on the bottom
of a coffee knock bin

Blurring the Lines

good and evil,
two warring tribes,
can't be told apart,
by the tint of their flags,
by the number of
stripes stitched to their uniforms,
by the gestures or grimaces
fastened to their banners
proud casting at us their explicit
shadows as solid as a shroud,
neither can they be
easily categorized, like birds, like frogs,
or like lush plants, as they categorically
defy the tables' most learned confines,
and all that we can do, if I recall,
is to rely on the lines
that too many dare to cross
like a child armed
with a fistful of crayons
bright

Peace Offerings

I know a thing
or two
too big to be swept
under the rug

I know what happened
to the wreckage of the last
spring, long in its
death spasms

I know what they
have done in the name
of applause
of sorts

I know what gives
you the sense of
purpose
in me long gone

I know that we are
the quaint reminders
of feelings that
cancelled each other out

I know that you pose
as a pallbearer
of truth, though the coffin
on your shoulder seems too light

The Death of Subtlety

a punch in the face appears to have
supplanted an old-fashioned slap

as a form of feisty farewell
and goodbye; a kick in the gut,

that new air kiss blown
across one's vital organs,

now a norm, is soon to be
missed when a fresh fad

will make itself at home
in the dome of our culture

by that time most likely
already gone

Meditation

Surface Tension

I no longer recognize
my reflection caught
in the convex mirror
of a coffee

pot, immured there
and bulging there—
a table contortionist
without a cause;

no longer can I
recognize the edges of my
teeth backbiting
those of a lustrous knife;

no longer can I
trace any likeness to me
in the crude rendition
of my jaw

trapped
in the potbelly of a spoon—
a mensal Jonah held hostage
next to a jelly jar;

and no longer can I
recognize myself
in the specters of her
eyes

disfiguring me
and twisting me more
than any funhouse mirror
would dare to try

Our Path into Night

a flighty fleck of the nightly pallor
found its way through the window,
wistful and open wide,
right into our life
full of candor

or so we thought

in it waltzed
between you and me
then it spiralled and pirouetted
unfettered by
anything

of this world

inches below the ceiling it hung
reluctant to land, reluctant to touch down,
like the mistletoe that overstayed
its festive welcome
for far too long

and far too kind

and I wondered
if it would find its way out,
if it would leave us alone, intact,
or rather stay around
till morning at least

A Poor Dancer Disturbed

every day I retrace
the failing footsteps

of my fingers
and fingernails

on the tablecloth
as I urge my hand

to meet yours
in an impromptu rendezvous

under the full moon
of a kitchen lamp

on the chequered dance floor
of our kitchen life

The Shadow of a Doubt

behind the flame
in your eyes
I see another one
hidden there like

a suitcase stuffed
into the back
seat of a car
during a family trip

that I can't reach,
that I can't
unpack without
unbuckling the seat

belt and letting go
of the wheel
and losing control
of all there is

to lose

High Hopes

beating its wings against
the cage of the azure
a little bird hopes
to be free

how I hope that
she will greet
me kindly today

but again she greets me
with a snarl

Leaves

never tell me
that you feel
the phantom
pains

of the amputated
leaves fallen

on the closed lid
of our life
together

never tell me
that you fear
the indifference
of the sky

and that's the only
reason why you
take hold of
my hand

so long uncared
for

The Upper Hand

the colon of the moon
reflected in the lake makes
me ponder the plight
of the Knave of Spades,
the printed wonder; two
opposing figures pinned
to a card, a case of dichotomy,
two twins torn apart since birth;
so am I, and my ears, two copies
of the same, two hands and two legs
moored to one name, there are
more examples of this rule,
more or less banal than that,
but I carry around with me
one version of this world
that I will never
give up

A Recipe for Solace

divide eternity,
that slice of a secret obscure,
by human intellect to get
the square root of brilliance

pure; look into the future,
these binoculars used
the wrong way, to see
the fingerprints of legions lost

in the fray; listen to the lament of leaves,
that dirge crooned every fall,
to hear the whine shrill
of felled tree trunks

once tall; take a pinch of this,
add a tad of that, and remember
that some have slept longer
than we live and still don't wake up

In the Shadow of a Clock Tower

I spent my childhood
in the shadow of a clock
tower dictating the rhythm
of the day, ruling over time, calling
the hour, ordering everyone
around, not only me, but also
my mother, my father,
even a homeless hound roaming
the streets, the back alleys,
our backyard; the clock
tower itself acting
as a magisterial clock's hand;
its shadow sketching a circle
after circle, all concentric
and grand, gliding noiselessly
over our heads akin
to tiny digits, those dimples
haunting a clock's face
and chin; a shadow
playing tag with us,
a clock within a clock,
time within time;
but now I have grown up
and moved away from
my family home, yet still
I see this shadow
as part of my own

In Loco Parentis

the fingers find my father's face,
they touch his skin now sallow

and graze against his freckles
now akin to grain,

they play with his stubble,
now eternal, that used to last

just a day or two at the most;
but now, black and white,

hiding under the veil
of photographic film,

all this is laminated
for ages to come;

a fish in the frozen
pond

The Anatomy of Weather

an autumn wind,
that murderer of leaves,
uncaught, its wanted poster
has been printed and
lost, pillages the boughs
ravages the twigs, gives paper bags
a spin, or two, on a parking lot;
each empty branch
a cemetery of sorts,
snowdrifts of leaves
are shaken and shoved around
like pawns on the palm
of a chessboard; is it true what
they say that it can smother a candle
and spirit one's last breath away?
the fallen tree seems to agree,
its upturned roots, bare, dangling,
revealed—legs devoid of a skirt;
for me, however, it's a breezy chap
toying with the propeller tiny
on a child's cap

Seeking Refuge

a dent in the pillow,
this intimate valley,
snow-white and
unblemished,
in which till recently
your whole world
was accommodated,
all your dreams and desires,
hiding in your head, half buried
in a soft flood of folds,
like a stone playing hide-
and-seek in the snow; a dent
that you carefully
smooth out every dawn,
every day, as if in shame,
as if fearing that
you are doing something
somewhat wrong, although
you know well
that it will return
when the darkness
calls you again
soon

The Monochrome

show me the night
of your past draped across

the canvas of a photograph
unretouched, black and white,

the binary world and we
reduced to its binary rules,

the kingdom of gray shades
and hues; you can color
my doubts, if you like,

take off some of that varnish,
the monstrous monochrome,
peel it off

and see what's beneath it;
don't listen to the nagging
of the clocks,

those ungodly gods looking down
on us from the tall towers,
the modern mountaintops lofty

and detached, pushing us back
back further into the past

Fallen

when I see a star
tumble down the top
shelf of the early dawn

so early, in fact, that the sun and the moon
still compete for room
on the barely awakened sky;

two players in the celestial
hopscotch game;

when I see a star sketching
and scratching a line
as fine as the smile
on a dingy dime,
an aerial arc above
my hands and my sins,

all sinewy and strong,
I hope
to pick it up, yet not
before making a wish that it stayed
where it was; there I was,
that is, above

your eyes akin
to no vacancy signs
on a parking lot; at night,

streets burn with billions of suns
blazing and blinding me
from their stems tall,

or is it only the reflected light,
reflected from you or
from me

or from anything that
makes me feel gravel sharp
under my palm when I fall

The Color of the Night

what is the color
of the night
you may ask, just as I
used to ask

my wife, as I gazed out,
out of the window
out of the tar pit
of my life

through the screen
of glass still bright, still
radiating the warmth
of the day

past, that's for sure,
but still amassed
in its bones glazed,
like a husband's smile

entangled in the threads
and loops of a widow's veil;
and there I saw
the topography of the land,

still untouched,
still intact,
under the unclothed
sky, and yet different

at the same
time, as if hidden
under the cozy coverlet
of snow, as if swept

under a rug
effacing the world,
though pitch-black;
and I felt the fear

of the dark returning,
after an absence
long, returning to me
like a friend

unwelcome
and unlonged-for, but I still
hoped that it won't last,
that, like a sickly child,

it won't survive
the rigors
of the night

The End of the Day

the collapse of the day
is no different,
they say, from
the nation's prompt fall,
from civilization's last chapter,
from the cave-in of the house
of cards not followed
by living happily
ever after

and yet

I feel
even though
the sense of touch
and a menagerie
of other senses have long
deserted me as if
I were a shuttered house
or an island long shunned
in an archipelago
of masterful misery
or a rudderless ship
bound

for nowhere
from nowhere

but I feel, I still can feel
that there, beyond
the horizon's taut smile,
above the aquiline nose
of a slow sundial lies,

for it must lie
somewhere,

a place
where we will meet;
look me up if you reach it
first

Posing for Frost

I was once a model
for frost,
for his paintings
sadly lost now

I saw him dip a brush
in the snowy lane,
then blur the landscape
and I got lost

on the canvas
of a windowpane, my
thoughts flowed free
of his reign cold

erased by his touch,
my breath would quickly
wane on this glass
ever-pale

Flightless Icarus

the empty seashells of summers
past, the casings once fired

and lost, loiter often
on my memory's shore,

mellow and mild,
that brought me no

comfort, no cheer, no calm;
many have looked, they say,

into the face of the sun and lived
to tell the tale, but I, in turn, kept my eyes

low, lowered for the sake
of my myopic gaze, or so I told

myself

In the Park

little streets and little squares,
little alleys winding all around;
two dogs fighting for every inch
of a stick; an infant giving a learned
speech from a stroller deep;
crows, like vultures, regarding
amblers from above; children
stomping boldly on the bones
of the last fall; a fountain, still dry,
a refrainer forced into abstinence
by winter's cold insolence; and I,
on a bench, falling for this diminutive
allure—this cruelty in miniature

Carte Blanche

behind the pall
of a morning mist, the sun,
ending its early tryst
with the wilting milky way,
reassembles a semblance
of a day scattered
across the sky, the ground,
shattered the other night
when the caesura of a dusk
put an end to its antics wild,
now its humble husk hums
with a wealth of wings, with
a myriad of mouths urging
me, pleading with me, to give
another chance to those
who wronged me

again

Correcting the Watch

two hands
locked in
a dance unaware

of the power they
wield over the paleness
of our hair,

over our expiration
dates, over a loaf of bread
not yet stale,

over the hue of our
despair, over plumy patches
of mold still unbudded,

but when you come to correct
their course, like a pilot
turning a plane around,

without regret or remorse,
by hurrying them up or
by slowing them down,

by synchronizing them
with the dictates of
the cocky clock

tower, you commit
the greatest
indelicacy, for

the communion of clocks
is not to be watched
in public

The Tiniest Show

a nimble coin
tap-dances on the bar
but the world
never stops to watch

Caring for Thought

not too many care for thought;
without an iota of inner

life they cannot be bothered,
nor stirred, nor riled, nor hurt—

a cocoon weaved to spite reality
curt—or so they tell themselves;

immune to the irregularities
of life, they are, yet still

don't know,
just a swan half-buried in ice

The Pantomime of Trees

try to read
the panic pantomime of trees,
showing me things,
giving me signs,
issuing warnings wary,

like lighthouses long faded
in which the light
was put off
by the same motion
desperate that was supposed to

keep them safe,
keep danger at bay,
at least
as long as was needed
to keep them safely aflame

A Discovery

do some people even know
that they live in towns

covered
by the blanket of black

grids on a map,
and do they hold it against

the cartographer's
headstrong hand

that they thrive in the shade
eternal of these lines drawn

over and across their lives
and fates

The Fall

I have always wondered if
by reading a paper
upside down
held by a man
sitting

in front of you
on a morning train full
of commuters, of mothers, of fathers,
of bosses, of beggars, of secretaries,
of someone's aunts and someone's brothers,

of keepers of diaries written badly
those half-dead, caffeinated ghosts,
those converted drunks of morning light
trying to make the most of the square
inch,

or two, allotted to them,
you ran the risk of
making your whole world
fall down on its
head

Rigor Mortis of Spring

shallow shards of shattered glass
can hold no reflection, no image, no
pieces of the past, for that is what

a reflection is—a captive,
a memory of a moment
that no longer lives among us:

a smile that has segued into
a sneer; the first kiss that was followed
by nonsense not so dear;

and I, a barren receptacle,
immune to the spectacle of our time,
can hold no seed, no grain, no

crumb of current claptrap, like a once-
fertile field on which, in seasons past,
a blade of grass would raise a flag on a mast

The Dark Groove

the first wrinkle spoils my youth's
forgetful face even though

it's not an ancient comb, a pan,
or a broken vase discovered

in a turbid tomb of the past tense;
no longer in fine fettle,

I watch it with dismay; the shallow
rut on a vinyl disc that may play

a wave of sounds till then enchanted
in that groove light, when gently stroked

by a record player's playful needle;
but will this wrinkle, when touched

by my finger stray, set free
a mosaic of moments and memories

that has grown strange
even to me, even now

Ducks at Dusk

a pristine prism of pride
must be what
drives ducks to flaunt
a victory sign each time
they scale the sullen sky;

a pale phantom of pain
must be what
strips the sky of its hues
and shades each time
the sun sinks down the skyline;

a dull desire to depart
must be what
heaves in the heart
of a domesticated man
admiring ducks at dusk

A Change of Heart

no wrinkle will ever
mar its texture
brusque and brash,

never will it mimic
a forehead's affection for ruts or
a neck's fondness for folds, at least

so I've heard,
for the heart gets old
without ever growing old

A Candlelight Vigil

you might have heard
haughty herds declare
poetry dead,

surrounded by votive
candles, all alight;
a murder victim

with an outline made
of chalk drawn
all around it;

a noose pristine white, or
a crown, closing in, closing its
ranks; they declare it lying

on a catafalque
high, on a granite slab,
and we, the ones

carrying candles,
all alight as well,
can see

the flames flicker
and dance in our hands
unsuspecting still;

but is it only a playful gust
that has crept in here
and prances around

irreverently with open
disregard for all
that's holy and unholy,

or is it, by any chance,
the last sigh prolonged
by one not entirely dead

A Relic of Yesterday

a brushstroke on a canvas,
the acrobatics of a nib,

fingerprints lost in clay,
the flow of verses glib,

the marble fingers of figures past
touching us from beyond,

through the mask of motion's mist,
to lecture us on and on;

naturally immortal,
normally immune

to the ravages of wars,
to riots' truculent jolts,

to epidemics' morbid blemish,
art needs centuries to perish

The Flow

the passage of time,
that opponent proud,
moves the months,
pushes the days

around and minutes,
marching to its commands
heady as if heading
to an exile

timely in conditions
dire on the carousel of a clock
spinning round and round,
every day; every night is

a faithful facsimile
of its cousins past,
long gone and turned
into dust draped in black;

and I wonder while
trying to guess,
trying to forestall
his next move

in a preemptive attack,
I wonder if others,
whom I meet and see
only for moments brief,

who have lives,
lives to speak of,
and true troubles
to bewail,

are not making
a better use of all
that time and of all these
moves

that slip through my fingers
that I cannot close
while holding a book
that I cannot lose

The Old Age

on her deathbed, that cradle
of doom, a mother asks her boy,
when was the last time you cried,
my son

in a delivery
room

Passing

I bet you can't
remember
even if you
try

the last time a shadow
that you cast
showed correct
time

Trial by Fire

flame after flame
the heat passes on,
a miniature relay race,
a wildfire in micro
scale, a form of
remembrance,
a convention of candles
in the naked nave,
a blazing bullet list
of things, of persons, of sins
never to forget